Whether it's a day out visiting somewhere new and having a picnic, or a longer period travelling by land, sea or air to a place far away, it's holiday time!

This picture book, with a simple story, will conjure up all sorts of memories and give lots of opportunities to talk with young children about many different things relating to holidays.

British Library Cataloguing in Publication Data
Bradbury, Lynne
    Holiday time.
    1. Vacations – For children
    I. Title   II. Lobban, John
    306'.48
    ISBN 0-7214-9588-5

First edition

Published by Ladybird Books Ltd Loughborough Leicestershire UK
Ladybird Books Inc Auburn Maine 04210 USA

Printed in England

holiday time!

written by LYNNE BRADBURY
illustrated by JOHN LOBBAN

Ladybird Books

It's time to go on holiday!
Let's get ready. What shall we take?

All the bags are packed.

Have we forgotten anything?

Where shall we go?

Some people
go to the sea.

Some go to
the country.

Some people like towns and cities
with interesting things to see.

How can we get there?

By car...

or coach.

By train or plane.

By boat or even bike.

This looks like
hard work!

Load up the car and we'll be ready to go.

Will there be enough room for everything?

Down at the bus station
— here comes the coach.

How many people are waiting?

...*ours!*

 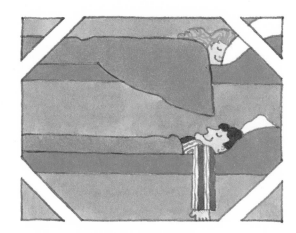

People eat on the train
...and sometimes sleep on the train.

What can you see through the window?

The airport is busy.
How many planes can you see?

Fasten your seat belt
ready for take off...

We're high in the air.

''Would you like something to eat?''

At last we've arrived!

But where shall we sleep?

Some people stay in hotels.

Some have a caravan...

or live on a boat.

Some stay in a house or flat.

And some people
like to be outdoors
and live in a tent.

It's a lovely sunny day.
What shall we do?

We could play on the beach…

swim in the pool...

go for a ride...

and have a picnic.

Today it's cloudy and cool.
What shall we do?

We could go for a walk…

have fun in a big park…

and eat in a café.

Today it's raining.
What shall we do?

We could go to a castle
and see the dungeons!

Explore a museum…

take a ride
on a train…

and hope that
it's sunny
tomorrow!

The holiday is nearly over.
What shall we take back?

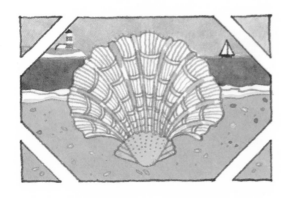

A shell from the beach.

A doll from the shop.

A balloon from the park.

A postcard from
the museum.

A pen from
the castle…

and a present
for Grandma.

It's time to go home.

There'll be lots of
things to tell
our friends.

Where shall we go
for a holiday next year?